THE 5 PILLARS

Five Actions to Build Your Network Marketing Business

ERIC AND TAMMY WALTON

The 5 Pillars
Five Actions to Build Your Network Marketing Business
By Eric and Tammy Walton

Published by SkillBites Publishing

ISBN-10: 1-942489-77-3
ISBN-13: 978-1-942489-77-1

TABLE OF CONTENTS

DEDICATION

This book is dedicated to the amazing people in Oiling the Gears! This team consistently pulls for each other as we all journey on the road to Diamond.

ACKNOWLEDGMENTS

Thank you to:

Kristin Warnaca who helped pull together the first presentations and helped with research, ideas, and words. Kristin, you are the BEST!

Andrea Johanson, whose editing brought new insights to the 5 Pillars!

Judy Weintraub and the incredible publishing team at SkillBites for putting up with me and getting the book over the finish line.

INTRODUCTION

Our goal with this book is to demystify the Young Living (YL) essential oil business, as well as to provide a foundation and structure on which a thriving business can be built. We're often asked HOW to be successful with Young Living. People say, "Just tell me what to do, and I'll do it!" The truth is, success in this business is based on some simple principles and activities.

We've identified five crucial building blocks that EVERY leader MUST do regularly. Regardless of your rank within our company, the activities are the same. This book is designed to help you get started building your business to Diamond by providing some blocks that you'll need.

What are those building blocks, those principles? They're the 5 Pillars: Share, Follow-Up, Educate, Serve, and Build! These pillars are the foundation and support upon which a healthy, thriving business is built. When you use these 5 Pillars on a regular basis, your business will start to move, gain momentum, and become an engine that won't stop!

Each chapter will go into greater detail about one of the 5 Pillars, but what do they look like in brief?

1. **Share** means to express your passion and love of the oils with those you connect with each day.
2. **Follow-Up** means to reconnect with people you have talked oils with, as well as with your current customers and business builders.
3. **Educate** means you continually learn more about the oils and the business yourself; then you share that knowledge with your team and customers and teach them to do the same.
4. **Serve** means to have a customer service focus while adding value to your customers and team, as well as helping those in need with their oil or business-related challenges.
5. **Build** means to develop your business builders, leaders, and team, supporting and equipping them in what they want to do with their business.

Focus your activity on these 5 pillars every day, every week, every month, and you'll build a very successful business. ***Even if you only have an hour a day to invest into your business, using these pillars in a focused and intentional manner will help you to move your business forward.*** **The key is to be consistent with your effort every week and to never give up!**

We want to reassure you that no matter your personality or skillset, you can be successful with each of these pillars. It's the PRINCIPLE that matters, not HOW you do it. So, if you like face-to-face meetings, great. If you want to connect via technology, no problem. The "how" is all up to you. As I've said already, there's only one road to Diamond—yours. Using these pillars in your own special way helps you find your unique road to Diamond.

This book is meant to be a management primer—easy to read, with lots of bullets and suggestions.

Each chapter will focus on one of the 5 pillars and have the structure of

- What
- Who
- Why
- How
- Teaching Others
- Resources
- Action Items

With tangible examples, resources you can use along the way, and action items to help you put the Pillars to use, you'll notice an immediate effect in your own business. While the content in this book will provide you with invaluable information, it's only when that information turns into knowledge that is APPLIED will your results be magnified and multiplied. So... do the action items at the end of each chapter and watch your business grow!

In addition to the 5 Pillars, there are themes and topics that weave throughout the book:

- **Ownership** is critical for success in this business quite simply because it's YOUR business—not your Enroller's, not your Sponsor's, not your Upline's... YOURS! No one can put the 5 Pillar "bricks" in your road to Diamond but YOU.
- **Taking action** is the hallmark of a successful entrepreneur. Without action, nothing happens—period. Even a wrong action is frequently better than no action at all. Take action with each pillar, starting with the ones suggested at the end of each chapter.
- **Essential Rewards (ER)** is the cornerstone of sustaining customer satisfaction and continuous revenue. Enrolling in ER will change your customers' lives and provide you with an income stream on which to build your business.
- **Being consistent and persistent** is what it takes to build a business. Ask any business owner who has "made it" what their secret has been and the two common traits you'll hear repeated is that they worked their business every day and they never gave up.
- **Connecting with other people and building relationships** is how this network marketing business operates. Without other people, you

have no business. They're not just customers, but people! And...you can't help them if you don't connect with them.

- **One road to Diamond** means that YOU have to find your own way there. Don't misunderstand—there are many resources and people to help you on your journey, but ONLY YOU can decide which tools to use and which counsel to take that will work best for you and fit who you are as an individual.
- **Playing to your strengths** is the very best way to choose those bricks and know how to use them in your road.

Let's get started by digging into the first pillar—SHARE!

PILLAR 1: SHARE

> *"Nothing, and I mean nothing, happens in this business until we share."*
>
> *–Eric Walton*

What is Sharing?

Sharing simply means to express your love for Young Living (YL) essential oils and how they have helped your family achieve greater levels of health and wellness.

Sharing is the absolute starting point to building your YL business. If you don't share, you don't need to worry about the other pillars because you'll have no customers or prospects—you'll be done. Hmmm... so sharing is not just *pretty* important, ***it's the lifeblood of your business.***

Sharing is your opportunity to express your love and passion for our products and for people. After all, our company's vision is "To bring Young Living essential oils to every home in the world." There's literally only one way for that vision to be reached... We all have to share!

You must find the courage within yourself to open your mouth or put your fingers to the keyboard and share your oil story. Think of those items, places, or experiences where you just had to share or you would explode. Now, have that same passion and urgency for your oils and your business will get rolling. We'll discuss shortly different ways to share, but sharing always starts with you!

Who do you Share With?

It's too easy to say, "Share with everyone." While that's true, it's no way to run an intentional business. So, who do you share with?

- **Warm market**—These are your family, friends, associates, and other people you know.
- **Cold market**—This is everybody else... BUT let's get more intentional with this one. Pick a niche that resonates with you—one that you're familiar with or have experience with. Some examples are:
  - Millennial moms
  - Dog lovers
  - Single moms
  - Yoga lovers
  - And many, many more

- The more specific your niche, the easier it becomes to craft a message that will attract them.
- AND...You still need to pay attention to the people around you wherever you are. Everyone needs the oils—you can be the one to listen and help them.

Why Share?

The most credible form of advertising comes from the people we know and trust. Let's start with this amazing fact: In 2015, the Nielsen Global Trust in Advertising Report showed that 83 percent of online respondents in over sixty countries reported trusting the recommendations of family and friends. That's the highest rating by FAR.

There's a reason people like to know how many stars a product has on Amazon and read customer reviews before selecting which free app they'll download on their phone. Trusting other people's opinions and feedback about a product, person, or service has a huge impact on our decisions (including purchasing decisions).

Young Living has a simple phrase, "love it/share it," and we totally agree. There's nothing more natural than raving about a new movie you enjoyed, a book that moved you deeply, or a little hidden gem of a restaurant in your favorite town. We share the names of our hairdressers, CPAs, dentists, and more with our friends. We even set our loved ones up on dates with our other single friends. It's rewarding to play matchmaker with products, places, or people... usually they're thrilled and say thank you!

You are the CEO and owner of your business. Sharing is YOUR job and YOUR responsibility; no one else will do it. Sharing is the #1 place to begin your business, and if your sales volume isn't budging, it's time to get back to sharing. Even Royal Crown Diamonds personally enroll people regularly because we never know who our next "racehorse" will be or who needs our help!

If you don't share the products and business opportunity with people, don't post about it on social media, or host any kind of classes, or bring it up in conversation, then what are you really doing? You certainly aren't running a business. It might be wishful thinking or a fun, casual hobby, but building a true business requires lots of consistency in the simple basics, especially in sharing.

It all starts with sharing. It's your first action to take when you decide to do the business, and sharing is one of the basics that absolutely MUST remain a part of your daily activities throughout your business.

People WILL want to join. Make sure they know they can join with ***you***. Our products are so good that eventually, most people WILL want to purchase and join or even build a business. If *you* don't share, someone else eventually will, and then you've missed out on an opportunity to connect with someone you could have helped and who may be a rock star business builder. Always share!

How to Share

Be intentional and strategic about how and when you share. It doesn't have to be a formal class setting, but you do need to make a practice, a habit, and a lifestyle of sharing your passion everywhere you go and inviting people to take a look at the products and the business.

When choosing the "best" way to share, keep in mind two factors—using your strengths and being situational. What does that mean? First, choose the method of sharing that you're best at! If you excel in the classroom setting, then schedule a bunch of classes and keep at it. We know many Diamonds who got there by holding class after class and not caring if only one person showed up. Just keep teaching!

Second, you also need to be situational. Many times, the best way to share is to throw out a wide net using social media, letting a large number of people know about a new oil or a new supplement. Or you may be at the airport and you have the opportunity to share with just one person—the person sitting next to you. Be YOU and be sensitive to the situation you're in.

There are many different ways to share oils with people—there's no magic bullet (or capsule) for sharing. It's pretty straightforward:

- Connect with someone you care about. In fact, sharing is a way to show people how much you really care about them.
- Share the product/business with them (samples, online class, video, in person class, one on one, etc.)
- Help them get started
- Show them how to share with others
- Don't be afraid to mention Essential Rewards at this time—let your intuition guide you

We like to encourage you to:

- Play to your sharing strengths.
- Be willing to take risks, try new ways to share, and learn new skills.

Some ideas for how this might look:

- Meet face to face with someone over coffee, and bring samples. You can use the corporate samples or make your own, but it's a GREAT way to share and help them engage with the oils.

- Give hostess, baby, bridal shower, and teacher appreciation gifts with a little handwritten card. Get products into people's hands to try. Once they try them, they're much more likely to buy!
- Post a personal story on social media—BE AUTHENTIC; TELL YOUR OWN STORY. Don't just copy and paste what someone else writes. This is your free advertising space! Make the most of it as you connect with your warm and cold markets.
- Initiate a conversation with someone you don't know at the gym, grocery store, or doctor's office. Look for ways to meet new people and get out of your comfort zone. I know more than a few leaders who have signed up people at the airport and even in elevators.
- Use your oils EVERYWHERE; people generally like the smell and will ask about it. Put citrus oils in your water when you're at a restaurant and leave the bottle on the table. Offer to share some Thieves hand sanitizer before eating with friends, etc.
- Do an online Intro to Oils class and/or schedule at least one in-home class a month (more is better, if your schedule allows).

- Join new activities, such as a gym class or sport, and use your Deep Relief roller or Cool Azul gel in the locker room or before exercising.

When you're first starting out, it's beneficial to try several different ways to share. Find out what you prefer and what you're good at. Use other resources that have already been tried and found to be successful, including others' pictures and scripts. NOTE: *Please always give credit to the creator of the material you're using.*

When you've found that "special" way for you to share effectively, take the tools and make them your own. Tweak them to work best for you. And remember you HAVE to be consistent and share every opportunity you can!

Before we leave this pillar, it's important for you to understand how to have exponential growth in your business. Sharing is your #1 task, and your business can't grow without sharing. But... ***teaching others to share allows for multiplication to happen!***

Teaching Others to Share

- Focus on helping them identify their skills, talents, and gifts in sharing, then work with their strengths. You want them to use their own strengths, not copy you.

- Keep it simple (review steps of sharing from earlier).
- Use available resources rather than reinventing the wheel.
- Communicate that sharing does not need to be in person or through teaching a big class but can happen in many different ways, including social media.
- Send them online resources, tag them in a video, share samples, etc.
- Set reasonable expectations for when you share:
  - "NO" from a prospect generally only means "not at this time," not "no" forever.
  - No is also not personal; it's no to the *product* right now.
  - Some people need to hear the message seven times before they buy.
  - Share from the heart—everyone needs YL!

Resources

Here are some resources to help you and your team share more effectively:

- **Simplified Oiler** for daily social media picture and post suggestions, daily straightforward actions, online class outlines and unbranded photos, 101 class, business 101 class and more: www.simplifiedoiler.com
- **Check out the 101 script we have in www.downlineleadership.com/resources**
- The *Gameplan* book and workbook by Sarah Harnisch has a copy of a general 101 script and there are many other scripts available from other YL teams.
- Young Living catalog (run through the company history, Seed to Seal, product lines, and starter kits).
- Message/text an online class via Sway: https://sway.office.com
- The books *The Go Giver* and *Go Givers Sell More* by Bob Burg and John David Mann can be helpful.
- Project Broadcast for text services: https://www.facebook.com/groups/projectbroadcast/

Action Items

- Share with someone in a new way tomorrow. If you always use social media, then meet with someone in person. The purpose in mixing it up is to show that you can share every day in a bunch of different ways: you just have to listen to those around you.

- Set time on your calendar to share EVERY day this week. Make that a habit going forward.

PILLAR 2: FOLLOW-UP

"Diligent follow-up and follow-through will set you apart from the crowd and communicate excellence."

–John C. Maxwell

What is Follow-Up?

Follow-up is perhaps ***the single most important action*** that will grow your business!

Follow-Up means to contact those people you've connected with to see how you can help them with their questions and their essential oil journey.

This simple act of contacting people and reconnecting shows them that you truly care about them and their health.

Who do I Follow Up With?

Our business is all about relationships, and follow-up is the key to deeper relationships, trust, and influence. There are four groups to focus your follow-up energy on. You'll have different strategies for each. They are

- People who have expressed interest in Young Living essential oils (Potential Members).
- People who have bought a kit but nothing else (Kit Buyers).
- People who buy oils each month but are not involved in doing the business (Regular Customers).
- Business Builders and Leaders on your team.

Why Follow Up?

Here are some key statistics:

- 48% of people never follow up with a prospect.
- 25% of people make a second contact and stop.
- 12% of people only make three contacts and stop.
- **Only 10% of salespeople make 4 or more contacts.**
- 2% of sales are made on the 1st contact
- 3% of sales are made on the 2nd contact
- 5% of sale are made on the 3rd contact
- 10% of sales are made on the 4th contact
- **80% of sales are made on the 5th – 12th contact.**

Source: National Sales Executive Associate, https://www.nasp.com/

"To quote Shakespeare: 'All is well that ends well.' Except in sales, where you need exceptional follow-up."

–Jane Garee[1]

OK...don't get uptight here, we normally use the word "share" but the above quote used the word "sales" because follow-up is what professional salespeople do to make EVERYTHING happen and it applies to us. We are professional salespeople out to put Young Living essential oils in every house in the world!

Now, we're not just "selling kits." We're walking with people through a lifestyle of health and wholeness. "Get a kit and then quit" is not residual income, AND it's not making a difference in people's lives. So, our job is to follow up with people to help them have genuine changes in their health and wellness by using the oils. Without follow up, they will forget the oils or get distracted. By following up, you can guide them through the purchase and use decisions. Most times it is YOUR follow up that is the spark that lights their decision fire.

How to Follow Up

For potential members, we recommend ***immediate*** follow-up. Get their phone number or email and send them a courtesy note that same day saying how happy you were to meet them and talk about their health and wellness and that of their family. In this note, make sure they have several different ways for them to contact you back (phone number, email, Facebook/Instagram name).

If you don't hear back from them, use the 3-10-30 timing of days for follow up. That means you'll follow up in three days, again in ten days, and again in thirty days. If you're doing your math, that will be four follow-ups in thirty days. Remember—some people need multiple touches to take action, and this is a vital part of your job. Always remind them that this contact is about THEM, not you or selling the oils. It's not stalking; it's good customer service.

For kit buyers, ask them how they like to be connected with and use that method. Many people now prefer texting to email, for example, or are more responsive on Facebook Messenger or Marco Polo. We prefer contacting them on the day they buy their kit, then on the day the kit arrives, then seven days after their kit has arrived, and thirty days after the kit arrival.

Many leaders ask their new members if they would like to take part in a fourteen-day email campaign that focuses on one aspect of their kit a day, helping to give them a solid start on making the most out of their starter kit. Alternatively, they may invite their new member to participate in a fourteen-day challenge that will help them learn at their own pace.

Find good reasons to contact your kit buyers:

- Offer to open their kit for the first time with them and walk them through it.
- Help them research new oils and place their first reorder.
- Help them enroll in ER so they can enjoy even more Young Living products on a monthly basis.
- Share monthly promotions or sales with them.
- There are lots of newsletters out there—find one you like and share it or create your own.
- Follow your customers on social media and comment on their posts (don't just hit "like" and keep on scrolling; build relationships beyond the oils).
- Send an encouraging private message or handwritten note, samples, or gifts (think about your audience).
- And many, many more!

For your regular customers, it's good if you have a regular follow up with them at least once a month. This follow up can be in the form of a FB post, newsletter, blog, or mass text. You want to use a tool and message that captures all of the them at once. You can talk about new products, promotions specials, events, or other exciting news about YL or the oils. Your goal is to keep your regular customers informed as possible so their knowledge of available YL products continually grows. In addition, we suggest you make a personal connection with them at least once a quarter to see how they are doing and if you can help them with their oils, ER, or health.

For your business builders, your follow-up is about both the oils and their business. For the oils follow up, use the process we just described above with the regular customers. To help them with their business, it is vitally important that you intentionally develop your relationships with them by asking open-ended questions such as

- What is their WHY?
- What are their goals?
- What are their strengths?
- What motivates or demotivates them?
- What is the best way for you to help them?

Use the "Relationship Map" from the book *Downline Leadership* by Eric Walton and use what you know about your team members to create follow-up opportunities. What are they going through right now in their business that you can help with? Talk with them and ask lots of questions. Your help will come from their answers to these questions.

You can only follow up if you know who "they" are, so collect data! It doesn't matter if they're prospects, kit buyers, or business builders, get as much information about them any way you can and write it down. Over time you'll create your own follow up process. It may involve using

- Post-it Note reminders
- Collecting and filing business cards
- Calendar reminders
- Journal/notebook for lists and to keep track of contacts made and notes on conversations
- Phone reminders and apps
- Spreadsheet tracker
- Relationship Map
- Customer Relationship Management (CRM)

Don't forget to ask them their preferred way of communicating. Use the data collection method you're most comfortable with and the one you're most likely to use consistently. In spite of what you may think, people WANT to hear from you. If they don't, they'll tell you, and if they don't tell you, keep on connecting!

When following up, be interesting, be memorable, be funny/cute, be real, be genuine, and have it be about THEM. Use the phone whenever possible. While our millennial generation may *say* they don't want to talk, all of us really do.

Be bold and have courage to overcome your fears. Don't let the following statements stop you or become part of your self-talk.

- "But I don't know them."
- "I couldn't possibly send them a note this soon."
- "I can't call them... I'll just send them an email."
- "I don't know what to say."

Here are some more tips to help with follow-up:

- BAMFAM: Book a Meeting From a Meeting. This is an excellent way to avoid the awkwardness of trying to track someone down to make an appointment. While you are in the first meeting and you have their attention (dropping off a sample, ending a class, etc.), set a meeting RIGHT THEN for the NEXT meeting. "Let's get a time scheduled now to reconnect after you have a chance to try these samples. How does late this week look for you?" This is especially important when people order their starter kit. Get an unboxing appointment set AS THEY ORDER, for seven to ten days after. That way it's already booked, and you don't feel like a stalker. You can do an unboxing with them in person or via Zoom, Facebook Video, FaceTime, etc.
- Use Text, PM, Care Calls.

- Send monthly promotions/newsletters.
- Send Happy Mail:
  - handwritten notes
  - gifts/samples

Pro tip: automate this process as much as possible. Prewrite or use our "About to go inactive" and "Welcome" notes, which you can find in www.downlineleadership.com in the Resources section. Personalize it for your person and your personality, but set yourself up for success by making it easy to get it in the mail/sent as quickly as possible.

> "I have a simple philosophy: I follow up ***as many times as necessary*** until I get a response. I don't care what the response is as long as I get one."
>
> *–Seli Efti, Founder & CEO Close.io*[2]

Teach Others to Follow Up

- Again, focus on replicating results, not duplication.
- The HOW is less important than the WHAT.
- Share your templates for prewritten materials with your team so they don't have to reinvent the wheel.

- Model follow-up with them (let them see YOU follow up with THEM).
- Keep it simple and sustainable.
- Encourage them when they feel rejected/ ignored. Tell follow-up success stories. Praise efforts, not results.
- Some may like a spreadsheet; others may prefer index cards or calendar reminders.

Resources

Here are some resources to help you follow up more effectively:

- Follow-up spreadsheet in www.DownlineLeadership.com/Resources
- FITFUU, Asana, and Trello are CRM apps that help with follow-up and contact management.
- Google calendar reminders.

Action Items

- Make a list of the people you need to follow up with (prospects, members, etc.) and write it down in a system that works for you. If you don't know a system to use, then just write the names on a piece of paper or in a notebook. If you're more analytical, create a simple spreadsheet for follow-up.

- Follow up this week with everyone on your list and make it an ongoing practice!

PILLAR 3: EDUCATE

"I am still learning"

–Michelangelo, age 87

What is Education?

Education means to share information with others that will help them gain a greater understanding of the oils:

- How they work
- Where they came from
- How to use them
- How to order them

Education also means sharing information on how to run a Young Living business:

- Understanding the compensation plan
- Understanding organizational structure
- Recruiting other business builders
- How to promote the oils and the business
- How to lead your team

Jared Turner, president and COO of Young Living, recently said there's a huge market for essential oils. You know what? There is! People are seeing essential oils everywhere, but they don't understand their benefits, haven't used them before, and don't know *how* to use them. So, what are we to do? Educate them!

Start by recognizing that NO ONE knows everything about essential oils, so we all need to learn. Gary Young spent his lifetime learning, exploring, experimenting, and teaching. To be a constant learner, it takes humility as you have to acknowledge that you don't know everything. Growing a YL business is a journey of ongoing learning!

Where do you begin? Start reading, watching videos, and talking to others. Then you have to do something quite challenging—you have to have the courage to share with others what you've learned. Even though you yourself don't know everything, share what you DO know. Even if you only know about one product, you can share that product with someone else!

This is especially important for our "detailed personalities" who want to know every product before they teach anything. Instead, start with that one oil that made a difference for you, then get to know the oils in your Premium Starter Kit. Use your oils and develop your own stories. Use reference guides, apps, etc. Learn something new every week, and share it.

Expand your knowledge to other product lines as you have fun and experiment with new products in Young Living's varied lines. Experimentation works better when you're educated, so when you've discovered a new product through your research, try it out and develop a personal story of your own.

Our lives and the lives of our family gain value as we find new ways to live healthier. That takes education, which is why EDUCATION is a key pillar, and absolutely "essential" to your business success and your life!

Who to Educate

The categories we discussed in the last chapter still apply this week, with one addition...

- Yourself—It all starts with you! You have to be committed to a life of learning. This adds value to you and to others!
- Prospects need to know you do this as a business and that you're a resource for knowledge and support.
- Regular customers need broader education so they get comfortable with trying new products.
- Kit buyers need deeper product education so that they become REPEAT customers, not just one-time kit sales.

- Business builders need more education on the comp plan, structuring their team for success, overcoming objections, limiting beliefs, and leadership.

We're going to focus primarily on customers and kit buyers in this chapter to give you more depth of knowledge and resources. You can use the same education with prospects, but their needs tend to revolve around the kit and single oils or blends. We'll be covering business builders in future pillars.

Why Educate?

In the last pillar, we took away the fear of words like sales and selling. We're going to continue with that in this pillar. Remember how 80 percent of sales are made on the fifth-plus follow-up attempt? Remember 90 percent of people STOP ASKING before they get to number five? This alone should get you motivated to educate people over and over again!

We also said that success in Young Living is not about a one-time kit sale but rather a *lifestyle* of health and wellness. EDUCATION is where we make that transition and connection. If you're excellent at sharing and follow-up, you'll enroll a lot of people, but it will be a revolving door with tons of one-time purchases without education. This is a recipe for exhaustion and frustration. EDUCATION, combined with good follow-up and service, transforms a casual 100 PV kit purchase into a dyed-in-the-wool, raving fan who orders 300 PV+ per month FOR LIFE.

Here are some interesting facts we've discovered:

- Unless you're a high and consistent enroller, it's likely that more than 85 percent of your check comes from repeat business.
- Young Living has over 300 products. It can be overwhelming. We need to help people simplify and focus. How? Through education!
- It is 6-7 times more costly to acquire a new customer than to retain an existing one. – *Bain & Company (www.bain.com)*. This means that by educating our customers, we significantly increase the chance that they'll continue to use the oils!
- A 5% increase in customer retention yields an increase in profits between 25%-95% –*The Loyalty Effect*[3]
- Customer loyalty is the single most important driver of growth and profitability. – *Harvard Business Review*[4]

Essential Rewards (ER)

- If the vast majority of our business comes from repeat customers, then ER has to be one of the most important tools! I recently heard from a Diamond that between 86%-89% of their monthly Overall Group Volume (OGV) comes from ER customers. Doesn't it make sense, then, that we spend a lot of time teaching on ER?
- Essential Rewards is the bread and butter of our business on both the oil side and the business side. On the oil side, what better way is there to ensure that your family has consistent access to oils than ER? When we educate people about ER, we start from the oil side. Starting from the oil side ensures a consistent supply of needed oils. It gives members the opportunity to get extra oils for free that they might not have tried otherwise. When you've really begun to live an oil lifestyle, you need ER to make sure your monthly needs of supplements, personal care products, AND oils are met. Educating people about the products and the diversity of the product offerings will help them see the value and wisdom of ordering monthly!
- Then there's the business side of ER. ER is one of the most powerful business building tools in your arsenal, and it's imperative to consistently

educate your team on its benefits. As customers join ER, there's a consistent flow of orders supporting your OGV. Use your intuition to know when to introduce ER into the discussion, but we've learned to do it earlier and earlier and in many cases we now introduce ER at the time of the kit sale.

- PV Assistant is an incredibly useful tool for ER. We recommend that everyone use this tool. If your ER products are not available, PV Assistant puts another product in the missing product's place so your ER value remains above the minimum threshold you've set.

Remember that our business stability is built on REPEAT orders from the same members. Essential Rewards is the strength and health of your organization, which means that ER and PV Assistant are some of your most important assets.

How to Educate

Be constant and consistent in educating your customers and business builders.

Get curious first! Ask about:

- Their preferred style of learning (visual, auditory, etc.).

- Their personality types—because of personality differences, you'll find that some will connect more with particular YL educators than with others. Knowing their personality type will also help you to better communicate with and motivate your team members.
- Their driving needs/what brought them to YL (are they super interested in gut health or a specific product line, age range, body system?).

Then...

- Connect them to your resources (this could be YL, your upline, or your resources).
- Encourage them to try new products and share their experiences.
- Share the value of Essential Rewards.
- Teach them about PV Assistant.

Just as with sharing, use the education method you're most comfortable with and the one you're most likely to use consistently. This can be FB Live, prerecorded video, live classes, mini audio snippets on FB Voice Messenger, writing, etc. Don't think you have to do it like other people. Find the method that works for you and teach using that platform. You also don't have to reinvent the wheel. Consider supplementing your education approach with resources already created by other YL educators.

Mix the education up—try new things like Instagram stories or IGTV, for example! Keep in mind that people learn in a number of different ways (e.g., auditorily, visually, etc.), so mixing up the ways you educate will be beneficial for multiple reasons.

You do NOT need to be a full-blown science expert to provide value to your team! Tell them what you like and why, and help connect them to resources! Educating does not have to be hard, but it is important to do it.

Here are some other ideas on ways to educate your customers and business builders:

- Facebook Lives in your group/on your page
- Instastories/IGTV
- Marco Polo group videos
- Prerecord videos and post on YouTube/Vimeo/FB
- Podcasts
- Written product posts on social media
- Zoom classes
- Sharing posts from other leaders, YL corporate, YL blog, etc.
- Live in-person classes, workshops, rallies, etc.
- Sway classes
- 1:1 education

- Newsletters and Blogs
- Personal texts, PMs, IMs, Marco Polo, email, in-person meetings, Zoom calls, etc.

Teaching Others to Educate

- Again, focus on replicating results, not duplication. Helping others to find their teaching strength is key!
- Share your class outlines/scripts.
- Use the Three-class model (you teach, they watch; you teach together; they teach alone and you give feedback; then they're on their own).
- Connect them to resources so they can learn and grow their knowledge.
- Build their confidence in baby steps by giving them small nuggets of responsibility. Let them build their education muscle by giving them "a piece of the pie" and letting them teach part of a class, prepare part of the outline, close the event, etc. Ask them to do Facebook Lives in your group as part of an education series without having to be responsible for the entire thing, etc.

- Love on them, build up their confidence, and have them get feedback on their educational efforts whenever they can.
- Use the feedback to build their skills and find out where they feel stuck/feel strong.

Resources

- *Essential Oils Desk Reference* (EODR) or *Essential Oils Pocket Guide* (EOPR) by Life Science Publishing. Please note that these resources are now also available as a mobile app.
- Get familiar with Virtual Office resources:
    - Use your Dashboard daily and familiarize yourself with each of the links.
    - Check out Member Resources and YL University, and direct new members there as well.
    - Learn the rank qualifications. Check out Monique McLean's videos on the compensation plan at http://ohmyoils.com/videos/comp as an additional resource.
    - Track your OGV—current and what is still scheduled to process.
    - Monitor your personally enrolled. You'll gain valuable information on ways you can provide

stellar customer service and indications of conversations needed regarding ER enrollment and/or business building.

  - Essential Rewards—know it and be able to explain it, as well as the PV Assistant option. (If you're on ER, you *need* to have PV Assistant set up!)
  - Use Essential Rewards to try new products and learn more about YL's product lines.

Remember... you have to educate on the oils AND the business!

Action Items

- If you don't already own them, immediately buy the EOPR and EODR and begin studying them.
- Pick three new oils this week and research them. Start first with the oils from the kit, then your personal favorite oils outside of the kit, then expand from there. Do this for the next year!
- Try a new method of educating your team this week.
- Run a report on your group ER percentage and put a plan in place to increase it that involves educating your team on ER.

PILLAR 4: SERVE

"People don't care what you know until they know that you care."

– Theodore Roosevelt

What is Serving?

Serving our customers and our team is at the very core of running a business. I mean, we have no business without customers. In this chapter, we'll review some of the ways to serve your customers and some resources you can use.

Servant leadership is an action and an attitude. When one of your customers has an issue, it becomes *your* issue. Help them resolve it. By doing that, you model how to resolve future issues by themselves.

Servant Leadership has the customer/member's best interest at heart. People will continue to purchase and be loyal primarily because of YOU, not just because of Young Living. The way you treat them and their issues really matters. REMEMBER... Even though we have a great product, they have other options and we want them to choose YL and YOU!

Service Mindset

Your goal is to bring ***value*** to your team. These are YOUR customers and members. Service is about the good and not so good things that happen. It's about checking in with them and fostering the relationship. It's being proactive in asking if they have any questions, or need oil suggestions, or if there are any oils sitting in a drawer somewhere that you can help them find uses for so they're able to make the most out of the oils they have.

It's also about handling all of their challenges. NO, you did not cause every problem or missed shipment. NO, you did not foster or create a bad expectation. BUT, things happen, people misunderstand or don't listen. So... YOU have to serve them. If you won't, who will? Start thinking like a consumer of oils and think through how YOU would like to be treated; then do it!

Food for thought:

- These are YOUR issues.
- They are NOT interruptions.
- This is YOUR business, and service IS the heart.

Who do you Serve

- Customers and Members
- Business Builders and Leaders

Remember, your team of builders and leaders are your customers as well. What do they need from you to have more successful businesses?

> "The companies that survive are the ones that work out what they uniquely can give to the world—not just growth or money but their excellence, their respect for others, or their ability to make people happy."
>
> – Charles Handy in *The Search for Meaning*[5]

Set Healthy Boundaries When Serving

- Set work hours
- Communicate when you will be available
- Communicate your preferred method of communication and always ask for theirs
- Let people know how quickly they can expect a response
- Be accessible

- Be responsive
- Be a problem-solver and show them how to solve their own problems!

Tip: Make sure each member has access to a reference guide and/or Oily app, so they think "look first and ask second."

One of the biggest challenges in this business is finding balance between your life (kids, husband, job, YOU) and your YL business. Healthy boundaries are necessary in this business, which is why it can be wise to set work hours or "off" times (e.g., My phone is off from 4-8 pm, I don't answer the phone when we're eating dinner, I put my phone in airplane mode at 9 pm, I don't post or reply to questions in my group on Sundays, etc.).

Let people know the best way to reach you (please send a text rather than leave a voicemail, for example). Give a guideline on expected response times. We like to respond the same day, but others give a twenty-four-hour window. If you're unavailable, it's OK to say, "I'm at my son's game; I'll get back to you tomorrow morning." What you don't want to do is ignore people, because that breeds distrust.

Figure out what's best for you and them, but these have to be YOUR boundaries. Don't let anyone tell you what they should be! If you don't want to answer a customer call, that's your choice, but be a business owner and understand that our choices have implications and impacts on others. Own your schedule and communicate it. Communication with your members will make them feel valued and respected. Own the issues and help your members to own the solution.

How to Serve

Earlier we talked about having the heart of a servant leader and learning to serve in the good times and when there are challenges.

When things are going well, it can sometimes be the best time to serve. By checking in when things are going well, you reveal your heart. You are showing you care about them. Serving your team can be asking probing, open-ended questions to find out what's really working or what's not. Calling a customer about this month's promotion is not only a good example of follow-up, but it's also an example of serving them, especially when the promotion is in their area of interest. Asking how they're enjoying the oils in their kit allows you to ask about their family and other areas you might be able to help with.

If a problem does arise, be a problem-solver and solution-finder. Think creatively! You'll first want to acknowledge the problem your customer is having. Customer issues can be anything, including errors made by the customer themselves. The KEY POINT is to present the problem, solution, product, and YL in the best possible light.

Keep it personal. Think of them as your customer and think of this issue as having your personal reputation and name on the line. Make it personal to you because it's already personal to them. I know, you didn't make the mistake, but remember that the customer didn't either!

Go the extra mile to make it better, no matter what. This isn't always about a customer service issue; sometimes it's sharing a resource book, dropping off samples for someone in a pinch, having flip kits on hand, trading product when someone runs out unexpectedly, running reports in Oily Tools, etc. With business builders, this might look like showing up at their event and bringing flowers to acknowledge their efforts, helping them set up for a big tradeshow, loaning out your logo tablecloth, showing up at their big class to help with setup and sign ups, etc.

Be a voice of positive encouragement. There is always a way to rectify a problem. Get creative... even if YL can't help make it right, find a way to make them feel cared for and listened to by sending a personal note, putting a credit on their account to cover shipping the next time, etc. A little caring and service goes a long way in a world where customer service is often overlooked.

Even if you're feeling personally frustrated with a customer service issue, don't vent to your customers or members or downline. Talk to your upline instead, and brainstorm ways to help your members. If you're going to post in your Facebook group, don't complain. Simply ask for help and be appreciative of the help you receive.

Be proactive. For example, when you see an issue, don't wait until the last two days of the month to address it.

Follow up after you've served them to close the loop—check in to make sure they were happy with the results from member services or that they got what they needed. If they weren't happy, ask them how you could have served them differently. Remember that by following up, you show the person how much you care!

Love and Leadership

The table below illustrates different leadership traits (left column) and the corresponding servant leadership action (right column). The more we serve our team, the more they know we care and the greater their loyalty, trust, and appreciation will be.

Love and Leadership by Katelyn Willadsen[6]

Patience	Showing self-control
Kindness	Giving attention, appreciation, and encouragement
Humility	Being authentic and without pretense or arrogance
Respectfulness	Treating others as important people
Selflessness	Meeting the needs of others
Forgiveness	Giving up resentment when wronged
Honesty	Being free from deception
Commitment	Sticking to your choices
Results: service and sacrifice	Setting aside your own wants and needs; seeking the greatest good for others

> "Of all the things that sustain a leader over time, *love is the most lasting*. The best-kept secret of successful leaders is love: staying in love with leading, with the people who do the work, with what their organizations produce, and with those who honor the organization by using its work."
>
> – *James Kouzes and Barry Posner, The Leadership Challenge*[7]

Teaching Others to Serve

- Remind people of their ownership of the challenges.

- Model results (let them see you serving and experience your care)
- Share success stories.
- Praise Member Services and team leaders who step up to the plate and solve issues.

It's a servant leader's responsibility to provide resources so your team can run their business effectively. Here are some resources you might find helpful.

Resources

- Live Chat Help: We like to recommend live chat as the first resource for a member product issue. Encourage them to email themselves a transcript so they always have a record of the request, who they spoke with, and the details of the conversation. Show them a sample chat. I like to actually have them log into their new account and then do a test chat with live chat after their enrollment or during their unboxing meeting.
- Member Services: Be sure ALL your members have the Member Services number in their phone. Save it in your contacts (800-371-3515) and text it to all your personally enrolled when they sign up. If a need arises, offer to do a three-way call with them to member services. This shows your

investment in solving their issue but keeps them actively engaged in solving the problem with you and models how you speak with YL corporate staff.

- Silver, Gold, Platinum, and Diamond Chat/Phone Lines: When helping members address an issue through Young Living, use your rank phone line if you have access to one.
- Enlist upline support if you're not getting the outcome needed. Sometimes a simple card or phone call from a ranked upline leader apologizing for the hassle makes a world of difference.
- *The Starbucks Experience* by Joseph Michelli: Author Joseph Michelli spent two years figuring out how Starbucks was able to take a commodity product like coffee and sell it for several times the typical cost. His book is an overview of how Starbucks was able to grow and continue to delight customers over time.
- *The Nordstrom Way* by Robert Spector: *The Nordstrom Way* is a customer service classic about a company that built customer service deeply into its culture. The book is filled with excellent, detailed examples of the hard decisions that were made to stay true to that culture over decades. Early in the book, authors Spector and

McCarthy quote Nordstrom's internal newsletter: "We don't determine what good service is; the customer does." It's a good standard we could all use as we work to create the best customer service experience.

Action Items

- Reflect on your most recent customer service "save." Ask yourself what went well and if there were any ways that it could have been an even better experience.
- Follow up to close the loop on a recent customer need to see how it went and try to determine the level of customer satisfaction in how it was handled.
- This week, check in with at least five customers to see how they are doing and how you can help them with their oils (make this a weekly "to-do").

PILLAR 5: BUILD

"You can have everything in life you want if you will just help enough other people get what they want."

–Zig Zigler

What Does it Mean to Build?

In this chapter, we're going to discuss one of my favorite topics—"Building Up Leaders"—and we'll review why it's important to invest in business builders on your team.

The first four of the 5 Pillars were about running your business and how to do it better. Building up other leaders is all about leading your team and GROWING your business through multiplication. The lessons from the first four pillars help you sell more kits by sharing your story, helping members enroll in ER through follow-up, gaining new customers and helping them use their oils through education, and creating more happy customers through service. This results in growth through addition.

But when you use the fifth pillar, Build with your leaders, you enjoy the power of multiplication. Not only does your business grow, so do your leaders, and their leaders, and their leaders, and so on!

In the end, no matter how well you run your business, sell kits, and help customers, there will always be a limit to what you can do. That limit is YOU! Let's change that whole paradigm and build a team of amazing oilers who want to change the world and their future! The path to growing your business on an exponential scale is through others and their growth, AND the only way to do that is to build them up, empower them to grow their own business, and to help those in their downline to grow theirs! Once this cascading power of leadership and growth kicks in, your business is going to take off!

But, before you can develop others, you have to develop yourself! Be committed to your own success. If *you* don't grow, your team won't grow. Invest in yourself and your development, then develop others.

- Build your own leadership skills by interacting with your upline's Facebook group, joining in on conversations with your community as you all grow together.
- Attend trainings and seminars, taking careful notes and following through on your action items. Take full responsibility for your own success.

- Develop an ownership mentality.
- Make events like Convention, Diamond Bound, Accelerate, local, YL Corporate events, etc., a priority. Invest not only in your own product education, but also in leadership development.
- Join and/or lead a mastermind group.
- Take advantage of the "Downline Leadership" coaching, training program (new groups launch every quarter) and the *Downline Leadership* book from Eric Walton!

To help build leaders, you have to know what one is. Here are ten qualities of a leader:

- **Has Integrity**—Do what you say you will do and follow through!
- **Is Confident**—The number one problem in any Young Living downline is a lack of confidence and having self-doubt. Find your inner strength and model it!
- **Has Passion**—Have an excitement about life, family, business, the oils, and yourself. Be the energy in the room.
- **Inspires Others**—Show people that it IS possible! Find balance with your family and the business, and get it done.

- **Is a Good Communicator**—Be clear, concise, focused, interesting, and fun.
- **Is Able to Make Decisions**—Remember that the stone is easier to move in the right direction once it's moving, but much harder when it's stuck. Make decisions and move forward. In many cases, a bad decision can be better than no decision at all.
- **Is Highly Accountable**—Be transparent and open to others evaluating your performance and whether or not you did what you said you would do.
- **Knows How to Delegate and Empower**—You know you can't do this by yourself, so engage and involve your team. If you're alone, then get it done yourself until you have a team.
- **Is Creative and Innovative**—Make stuff up! Have new ideas! Conduct brainstorming sessions with your team to adopt new team ideas and directions!
- **Is Empathetic**—Care about people!

No one is a ten in all of these areas. Find the ones you're good at and get really, really good at them. If one of your weaknesses is holding you back, learn how to become stronger in that area.

Who do you Build Up?

Start with the leaders and builders you already have, then look for new potential leaders. Hidden in your downline and warm and cold markets are Diamonds!

- They might use your products already (and may or may not currently be in your downline) or... they might need extra income.
- Look for people who ask lots of good questions—the ones who seem genuine in their passion for the oils. Look for those who like to volunteer for team events. Invest into those who want to listen. Use the "Teach One, Share One, Empower One" approach to classes that was mentioned earlier. Watch carefully for signs of interest everywhere.
- Begin with two people: find two people who want to do the business with you. Help them make the oils a family lifestyle and the business part of their lives. That's all you need to get started!
- Share your story often with those who will listen.

Why Build?

The chart below clearly shows the importance of replication (which is your people sharing with more people, sharing with more people). This spreadsheet shows you what happens when you enroll two people a month for a year, as well as what happens when they do the same. The difference in the size of your group at the end of the year is quite astonishing! This should be the goal for each of us—enroll two people each month and help our downline to do the same.

The Power of Building Leaders

24 vs. 531,440

"Heart Centered Sharing" by Vicki Opfer[8]

Month	You Enroll	... OR ...	Total Number of People From Last Month (Old)		They Each Eroll 2 (NEW)		Plus Your 2 New People		New Total People in Your Group: Old + New + Your 2
January	2						2		2
February	2		2	+	4	+	2	=	8
March	2		8	+	16	+	2	=	26
April	2		26	+	52	+	2	=	80
May	2		80	+	160	+	2	=	242
June	2		242	+	484	+	2	=	728
July	2		728	+	1,456	+	2	=	2,186
August	2		2,186	+	4,372	+	2	=	6,560
September	2		6,560	+	13,120	+	2	=	19,682
October	2		19,682	+	39,364	+	2	=	59,048
November	2		59,048	+	118,096	+	2	=	177,146
December	2		177,146	+	354,292	+	2	+	531,440
Totals for Year	**24**								**531,440**

As Vicki Opfer explains, "We can *hope* that our product users will eventually share with others. Or, *we can learn the skills of teaching and* BUILDING UP LEADERS— let's help *every single one* of our downline members understand how to share with others and enroll them. This may include *our* learning how to *model* sharing to our downline members. And then helping them to teach their downline and so on."

While each of us only has a certain amount of time and energy, the COMBINED efforts of a team working together is multiplied exponentially. You may not be able to be in two different places at once, but with a team, you CAN!

Statistics show that if someone has just one person in their downline, they are twice as likely to order and half as likely to go inactive than if they have no one in their downline. Not only that, the more people they have in their downline, the more likely they are to order. And, of course, if they're ordering oils and other products more consistently, they will most likely significantly improve their health and well-being over time. It's a beautiful win/win.

How to Build Up Leaders

How do you build up other leaders? Leaders use their influence. But how do you get influence?

- Think like a coach—ask open-ended questions.
- Use your intuition.
- Help builders set realistic monthly goals and actions.
    - Help them to get their business started with the 5 Pillars.
    - Help them to set monthly goals—something tangible and actionable to shoot for.
- Use the Leadership Engine from the *Downline Leadership* book: Establish Credibility, Build Relationships, Earn Trust, and Gain Influence.

Role Agility

When building up leaders, you must understand what situational leadership looks like and how to use it. There are four main roles in leadership. It's important to be agile, meaning you shift between the roles quickly and at the right time, and it will take your intuition to know when to switch gears.

- **Director:** Tells them what to do. This is the most efficient and least effective leadership role. It can lead to a very dependent team if overused.
- **Teacher:** Shows them what to do. This is so helpful in YL! Take a few extra minutes with

your new builder and show them how to get their enrollment link, find the Out of Stock list in the VO, etc. If you're getting asked a lot of questions, ask yourself, "Have I done enough teaching?" This is critical for new business builders.

- **Mentor:** Shares with them what you would do. Uses statements like these... *I'm going to share with you what I would do. Here's a scenario I've experienced. Here's what I learned in structuring my team*, etc. This role is very relational and highly effective.
- **Coach:** Asks them what THEY would do. Uses open-ended questions to get to the deeper issues. This is the highest level of leadership. It takes the longest amount of time, but is the most effective and by far the most rewarding.

"Coach first, then pivot."

–*Eric Walton*

Teaching Others to Build Leaders

- Investing into your team brings the BIGGEST return of anything you can do.

- Focus on REPLICATING results, not duplicating exact steps. There are MANY ways to do this business.
- Use your intuition. Listen to their answers to your open-ended questions.
- Help them to use their own strengths to go after their marketplace.
- The most effective way to transfer your leadership and teach others is to show them, so... model leadership every day and in every way you can.
- This is THEIR business—they own it. When you're an OWNER, you stop waiting on your upline, you own your destiny, and you get it done. You stop blaming others or looking to have members placed under you by your upline. Instead, you go find your own leaders, empower them, and help them to really, truly own their own business.
- You will always have some people who won't work their own business and expect you to do it for them. Encourage them to find their niche, but don't waste time investing into them. Find the ones who want to build their own future.
- Getting to Diamond takes hard work, intuition, good decisions, and a solid team of builders. Keep building up others around you; it will ALWAYS pay off.

- In the beginning, teach your newbies, direct them, help them to find their strengths and how to use them. Build relationships with them and get 'em moving toward their own road to Diamond. When they're further along and starting to build their own teams, offer to spend time with them in the role of mentor and coach. You can't MAKE them participate in coaching calls, but use your relationship and trust to influence them to take some meetings with you. Your questions will help them find their own answers.
- Keep on explaining the four leadership roles and knowing through intuition when to use which role.
- When you ask questions, try to make them open-ended so you show them you care about THEIR answers, not yours.
- And this is key—try to take these personal relationships into the business realm. When you have enhanced the business side of your relationship, their respect and trust for you will grow. This enhances your leadership and your team will reap the benefits, so move on from talking ONLY about their family to talking about their business, and use open-ended questions when you do it.
- Remember, true leaders don't create followers; they create more leaders.

Resources

- Downline Leadership coaching groups (www.downlineleadership.com)
- *Downline Leadership* by Eric Walton
- 5 Pillars training system
- Open-ended questions
- All books by John Maxwell, especially *The 21 Irrefutable Laws of Leadership, Developing the Leaders Around You,* and *The Five Levels of Leadership*
- *Energy Bus & Soup* by Jon Gordon
- 12 Days of Diamonds Facebook group

Action Items

- Honestly evaluate where you spend most of your time in the four roles. Keep track for one week.
- Schedule a COACHING call with a member of your downline team who has leadership potential.
- Get the Relationship Map from www.downlineleadership.com/Resources and create a new tab for your current leaders and potential leaders. Intentionally begin to build relationships with each of them weekly.

CONCLUSION

This book is ending, but your work is just beginning! Here are some final thoughts to keep in mind.

Use the 5 Pillars daily, along with the resources in this book, to build your own road to Diamond. Most importantly, find ways to share that bring out your unique, special passion for people and essential oils!

Be intentional about your actions. Make plans, then do them. Make goals, then reach them. Do what you say you'll do and, trust me, people will want to buy from you, be on your team, and build a future with you!

Own your business and run it—don't wait for anyone else to do it. Do NOT play the victim. If something goes wrong, don't worry about who is to blame. Just fix it. If something doesn't work, then try something else. Take pride in your business and take responsibility for growing it.

Build relationships that matter. All 5 pillars are totally dependent on your ability to build relationships, to grow them, to nurture them, and to enhance them. The more relationships you have that are meaningful and impactful, the more the 5 Pillars work for you!

Keep at it! Don't give up, no matter what! Believe in yourself, believe in Young Living, believe in the oils, believe in your team, and just keep going. Use the 5 Pillars to build your own road to Diamond! The road to Diamond is not short, but it can be yours!

ABOUT THE AUTHORS

Tammy Walton has been with Young Living, helping people, changing lives, and supporting her family for over six years. She's been a Diamond for the past three years and leads an amazing team called "Oiling the Gears" (OTG). A mom of three incredible children, two of whom are Young Living distributors (one Diamond, one Silver), and a loving grandma of three, she lives with her husband and coauthor, Eric Walton, in Bend, Oregon.

Eric Walton is a leadership coach and speaker. His book *Downline Leadership* and corresponding Downline Leadership group coaching program have been used by almost a thousand Young Living leaders, including over 100 Diamonds, to improve their ability to lead their Young Living teams.

Check us out at www.DownlineLeadership.com for ways to purchase *Downline Leadership*, as well as many of the resources and tools mentioned in this book, and to learn more about the Downline Leadership group coaching program.

WORKS CITED

1 "To Quote Shakespeare: 'All Is Well That Ends Well'. Except in Sales, Where You Need Exceptional Follow up." *Jane Garee Sales Strategies*, janegaree.com/mid-week-sales-tweak-exceptional-follow-up/mwst-exceptional-follow-up/.

2 "Follow Up Like A Champ: How To Win Every Deal With The Amazing Power Of The Follow Up!" *LinkedIn*, LinkedIn, 30 Sept. 2019, www.linkedin.com/pulse/20140930234619-7006635-follow-up-like-a-champ-how-to-win-every-deal-with-the-amazing-power-of-the-follow-up.

3 Reichheld, Frederick F., and Thomas Teal. *The Loyalty Effect: The Hidden Force behind Growth, Profits, and Lasting Value.* Harvard Business School Press, 2008.

4 "Are Customer Loyalty Initiatives Worth the Investment?" *HBS Working Knowledge*, Harvard Business School, 1 Mar. 2004, hbswk.hbs.edu/item/are-customer-loyalty-initiatives-worth-the-investment.

5 Handy, Charles Brian. *The Search for Meaning.* Lemos & Crane in Association with the London International Festival of Theatre, 1996.

6 Willadsen, Katelyn. "How Servant Leadership Changed My Life." *The Odyssey Online*, 15 Nov. 2017, www.theodysseyonline.com/how-servant-leadership-changed-my-life.

7 Kouzes, James M., and Barry Z. Posner. *The Student Leadership Challenge: Five Practices for Becoming an Exemplary Leader*. The Leadership Challenge, 2017.

8 Heart Centered Sharing" by Vicki Opfer http://10000seeds.com/northgrovemarketing/wp-content/uploads/2015/01/HeartCenteredSharingVickiOpfer.pdf

Made in the USA
Columbia, SC
27 June 2019